William Berry Lapham

Family Records of Some of the Descendents of Thomas Besbedge

Besbedge

(Bisbee) of Scituate, Mass., in 1634

William Berry Lapham

Family Records of Some of the Descendents of Thomas Besbedge
(Bisbee) of Scituate, Mass., in 1634

ISBN/EAN: 9783337142278

Printed in Europe, USA, Canada, Australia, Japan

Cover: Foto ©ninafisch / pixelio.de

More available books at **www.hansebooks.com**

FAMILY RECORDS

OF

Some of the Descendents

OF

THOMAS BESBEDGE, (BISBEE,)

OF SCITUATE, MASS.,

IN 1634.

COMPILED BY WM. B. LAPHAM, M. D.,

Secretary of the Maine Genealogical and Biographical Society.

"Tell ye your Children of it, and let your Children tell their Children, and their Children another generation."—*Bible.*

AUGUSTA, ME.,
PRESS OF HOMAN & BADGER,
1876.

EGOTISM.

As a member of the committee, the labor of arranging the matter and superintending the publication of this pamphlet, devolved upon me. It was my purpose originally to print in full the historical sketch read by me at the Bisbee gathering, to be followed by the records of the descendents of Charles Bisbee, but after giving the subject careful thought, it seemed a better way to commence the Bisbee Records with the first American ancestor and bring them down to the present generation. This change has involved a great amount of additional labor and no little expense, but it will be of much more permanent value. and on the whole much more satisfactory. The records are not so complete with respect to dates as I could have desired, but they are as nearly so as it was possible to make them. A genealogy of all the descendents of Thomas Bisbee would require a large volume and contain several thousands of names. I have followed the trunk line down through several generations, dropping out names all the way, because the scope of the present undertaking would not admit of their being carried along. My aim has been to trace these lines until they diverged into Maine, and to follow them here, in order that all the descendents of Thomas Bisbee in this State may be able to trace their ancestry in an unbroken line, to their emigrant ancestor.

The delay in bringing out this pamphlet has been very vexatious and trying to me, but it has been owing to causes over which I could have no control. Over two years have elapsed since the gathering was had at Sumner, and at that time it was thought we could print the proceedings in six weeks. The delay is no fault of mine.

The small amount subscribed to defray the expense of publication has rendered it necessary to abridge the pamphlet somewhat more than was desirable. A more complete account of the proceedings at the family gathering, such as an abstract of the speeches delivered on the occasion, and the names and ages of all those who were present would be interesting, but this required space and involved expenses which had not been provided for. I also found it necessary to abridge somewhat the records of the descendents of Charles Bisbee, by leaving out in most cases the fifth generation, in order to keep the size of the pamphlet down to correspond with the amount pledged for defraying the expenses of publication.

I do not dare to hope that these records are free from errors, although I have taken great pains to render them so. Some of the manuscripts which I have copied were blindly written, so that it was almost impossible to decipher their contents. Those who have had experience will know how difficult it is to copy names and dates correctly, from a hundred letters, written by as many different persons, and will readily excuse any errors they may discover in these pages. With these few egotisms and excuses which seemed to be necessary, I commend these few Bisbee records to the care and consideration of such of this race as are interested to know something more of their ancestors, trusting that it may be preserved by them and passed down to generations yet to come.

WM. B. LAPHAM.

Augusta, June 10, 1876.

EXPLANATIONS.

The Roman numerals preceding a name refer to the place and number in the family. Figures are only used before such names as appear subsequently as heads of families. The large or fullfaced numerals refer back to their corresponding numbers, but of smaller size. Figures above and at the right hand of a name show the number of generations from Thomas Bisbee, the emigrant who is reckoned as the first. b. is the abbreviation used for born ; bap. for baptized ; d. for died and sometimes for daughter ; ab. for absent. A careful study of the numerals will enable any descendent of Thomas Bisbee to trace his ancestry through all the generations back to him.

A FAMILY GATHERING.

On the 9th day of June, A. D. 1874, there was a gathering of the descendents of Charles Bisbee at the old Bisbee homestead, in the town of Sumner. It could hardly be called a reunion, for few of those who assembled there on that day had ever met there before, and many of them had never before met anywhere. The invitation was given out by Capt. Lewis Bisbee, grandson of the patriarch, who now lives at the old homestead and cultivates the paternal acres. The invitation was extended to all connected with the family, either by marriage or consanguinity.

The weather was threatening in the morning, which probably prevented some from coming, but about a hundred and fifty of all ages had assembled before noon A large portion of them came from towns in the immediate vicinity, and a few from more distant places. The second generation from Charles Bisbee, consisting of his seven sons and two daughters, had long since passed away, but a few of the third generation were present, still more of the fourth, some of the fifth and one of the sixth.

The forenoon was spent in introductions, in looking over the old homestead and in social intercourse. At noon a picnic dinner was spread on the lawn in front of the old house. After dinner the company divided into groups or tribes, and it was found that seven of the nine children of Charles Bisbee were represented by their desendents. Each separate group was photographed by an artist, who was present for that purpose.

The company then assembled in the finely shaded and nicely kept cemetery situated near by, where repose the ashes of five generations of Bisbees. An organization was effected by the choice of Capt. Lewis Bisbee as chairman. Remarks were made by the chairman and by Hon. Sidney Perham and George D. Bisbee, Esq. A brief sketch of the Bisbee family of New England was read by the writer of this sketch, commencing with the emigrant ancestor and tracing the family down to those who were assembled on this occasion, comprising ten generations. At the close of the exercises it was voted that a committee be raised to prepare and cause to be printed an account of the meeting, and a genealogical sketch of the descendents of Charles Bisbee, and Capt. Lewis Bisbee, George D. Bisbee and Wm. B. Lapham were appointed the committee.

The day which proved to be one of June's loveliest, was very pleasantly spent, and towards night the company separated and returned to their respective homes, feeling that the occasion had been one of interest and profit.

Charles Bisbee, the common ancestor of those who assembled on this occasion, was born in Bridgewater, Mass., in 1726. He married Beulah, daughter of Rowse Howland of Pembroke, probably a descendent of Arthur Howland of Marshfield, and subsequently moved to Pembroke. At the close of the Revolutionary war, in which the father and his two oldest sons, Elisha and Charles, had taken part, there was an extensive emigration from the Old Colony towns to the wilds of Maine, or to the "Eastward," as it was then called, and Charles Bisbee, senior, was among the number of those who emigrated. He bought land of Benjamin Darling of Hanover, Mass., in a township in Maine, then called Sharon, afterwards Butterfield, and finally incorporated in 1798 by the name of Sumner. In the summer of 1783 he visited his land and put up a cheap tenement for his family. Buckfield had then been settled about seven years, but Sumner was a wilderness. Mr. Bisbee returned to Pembroke and spent the winter and in the following spring set out with his family for their new home. They sailed from Scituate harbor in a packet, and landing at Yarmouth, proceeded through the wilderness to Sumner on horseback, arriving on the 5th of June, 1784. He selected his land with good judgment, and with the aid of his seven stalwart sons he soon cleared him up a good farm. He suffered all the privations and hardships incident to pioneer life, lived to see his children comfortably settled around him, and to enjoy the fruits of his toil, and departed this life June 5, 1807, it being the twenty-third anniversary of the arrival of the family in town. His wife, Beulah, died Sept. 1, A. D. 1816.

The nine children of Charles Bisbee grew up to man and womanhood and all of them were married and had families. Their children settled in Sumner and the adjoining towns, and their grandchildren are widely scattered, many of them having made their homes in the far West. A record of some of these families may be found in the last part of this pamphlet.

The following letter, the original of which was obtained from Miss Lydia Ford of Hanson, Mass., who is a daughter of William Ford, may be of some interest in this connection. The letter was written by Elisha Bisbee, the oldest son of Charles Bisbee, and is directed to William Ford, whose wife was a Howland and a sister of Beulah, the wife of Charles Bisbee :

SUMNER, APRIL 29, 1803.

Dear Uncle :—I embrace this opportunity to inform you that we are all well as common. I have nothing new to write. It is a general time of health here. We have had a very moderate winter and as forward spring as we have had since I lived here. Bread and meat are plenty and cheap, and labor bears a very high price, and is not to be had at any rate. I was at the widow Child's lately ; all well. The Judge of Probate has done very extraordinary by the widow ; her dower would fetch twelve or fifteen hundred dollars, at least, and the Doctor's estate is likely to come out much better than was expected.

I have not had a line from you this many a day, and have done looking for any, but I am in hopes that my scribbling may stir you up so that I may know how you and our relations fare there in that old worn out country, and pray don't miss any opportunity of writing to me, as I shall take it very hard if you do.

We have had a very exceeding snow storm here. It began on Friday, the fifteenth of this instant, (April,) early in the morning, and grew hotter and hotter until Sunday, about noon, when it abated. The snow fell eighteen or twenty inches deep, and there is some of it to be seen now. It was far the smartest storm we have had for the winter past.

Our two oldest girls have got married and each of them have a boy. They married men of property, and are in a way to live if no misfortune overtakes them. Remember me to all that may inquire. Joshua Ford's oldest daughter is married and has got a boy.

ELISHA BISBEE.

To William Ford, Pembroke, Mass. To be left at Joseph Howland's.

BISBEE FAMILY RECORDS.

Thomas Besbedge,* the common ancestor of the New England Family of Bisbee, was one of those persons who came to New England soon after the landing of the May-flower pilgrims, in order that they might enjoy more per-fect religious freedom. There are many circumstances which go to show that he was a man of some wealth and position in the old country, and a man of influence in Ply-mouth Colony. The records show that he sailed from Sandwich, England, in the ship Hercules,† John Witherly master, with his wife, six children and three servants, and that he landed at Scituate Harbor in the spring of 1634. He had certificates from Thomas Warren‡ Rector of St. Peters' at Sandwich, and from Thomas Harmon, Vicar of Hedcorn, of his conversion and conformity to the orders and discipline of the church, and that he had taken the oaths of allegience and supremacy. He became a member of Lothrop's church, the first gathered at Scituate, and was chosen one of its first deacons. He remained in Scituate

---

* The various methods of writing this name, found in the old records, afford a good illustration of the mutations in English surnames. The following are some of the changes referred to: "Besbedge," "Besbidge," "Besbeech," "Beesbeech," "Besbitch," "Bisbe," "Besbey," "Bisby," and "Bisbee." The latter is now the recognized orthography.

† He came in the same ship with Elder Nathaniel Tilden, the founder of the New England Family of this name, and who became ruling elder of Lothrop's church.

but a short time, for in 1638 he bought a house of Wm. Palmer in Duxbury and moved there.   In 1643 he was chosen Representative from Duxbury to the General Court.   He was one of the grantees of Seipicon, (now Rochester,) but the grant was not accepted, and Mr. Bisbee subsequently moved to Marshfield, where his name appears on a petition to the General Court.   He afterwards moved to Sudbury, where he lived several years and died March 9, 1674. His will, dated Nov. 25, 1672, bequeaths all his houses and lands in Hedcorn and Frittenden, Old England, to his grandson, Thomas Brown, and makes two other grandsons, William and Edward Brown, executors.   The name of the wife of Thomas Bisbee does not appear upon the records of Plymouth Colony, which are equally silent respecting three of his children.   They may have died unmarried, or perhaps there may be an error in the record which gives the number as six.

The only children of Thomas Bisbee whose names appear upon the records are as follows:

1.   i *Elisha*, m. ——— ———
2.   ii *Alice*, m. John Bourne.
3.   iii *Mary*, m. William Brown of Sudbury.

1.   Elisha[2] in 1644 kept a ferry in Scituate, where Union Bridge now stands.   His house stood near the bridge, on the west side of the river and on the south side of the way.*   His house was a tavern.   Children:

  i *Hopestill*, b. 1645 ; m. Sarah ——— ; lived in Marshfield. We have no record of any children.   He died and his widow married a Lincoln.
4.   ii *John*, b. 1647 ; m. Joanna Brooks.
      iii *Mary*, b. 1648 ; m. Thomas Beals.

---

* Dean's History of Scituate.

5. iv *Elisha*, b. 1654 ; m. 1st Sarah King,* 2d Mary Bacon.
    v *Hannah*, b. 1655 ; m. Thomas Brooks. *4 1657 m 1687*
    vi b. ———; m. Jonathan Turner, 1677.
    MARTHA

2. Alice² m. John Bourne of Marshfield, and the marriage is the second recorded in the books of that ancient town. Children :

  i *Eliza*, b. 1648.
  ii *Thomas*, b. 1647.
  iii *Alice*, b. 1649.
  iv *Anne*, b. 1651.
  v *Martha*, b. 1653.
  vi *Mary*, b. 1660.
  vii *Sarah*, b. 1663.

3. Mary² m. William Brown of Sudbury, and had,

  i *Mary.*
  ii *Thomas.*
  ii *William.*
  iv *Edward.*

4. John³ married Joanna Brooks Sept. 13, 1687. He was married at Marshfield but moved to Pembroke and died there Sept. 24, 1726. His wife, Joanna, died Aug. 21, 1726. Children :

  i *Martha*, b. Oct. 13, 1688.
6. ii *John*, b. Sept. 15, 1690 ; m. Mary Oldham.
7. iii *Elijah*, b. Jan. 29, 1692 ; m. Sarah ——.
  iv *Mary*, b. March 28, 1693.
8. v *Moses*, b. Oct. 20, 1695 ; m.
9. vi *Elisha*, b. May 3, 1698 ; m. Patience Soanes.
10. vii *Aaron*, b. —— ——, m. Abigail ——.
11. viii *Hopestell*, b. Apr. 16, 1702 ; moved to Plympton and m. Hannah Churchill.

---

* Daughter of Thomas King of Scituate.

5. Elisha[3] was married to Mary, widow of Samuel Ba-
:on, and daughter of John Jacobs of Hingam, by Gov.
Bradstreet, March 25, 1689. He moved to Hingham and
died there March 4, 1715–6. His widow died at Pembroke.* Children:

     i *Joanna*, b. April, 1686.
12. ii *Elisha*, b. Feb. 28, 1687; m. Sarah ——.
     iii *Sarah*, b. Feb. 25, 1689.
     iv *Ruth*, b. —— ——; d. Feb. 10, 1713.
     v *Mary*, b. Nov. 7, 1700.

6. John Bisbee[4] married Mary Oldham† of Marshfield,
1710–11; lived in Pembroke and died there August 2,
1772. Children:

     i *Abner*, b. July 31, 1734.
     ii *Mary*, b. Oct. 28, 1736.
     iii *Elizabeth*, b. Sept. 20, 1741.
     iv *Sarah*, b. March 9, 1744.
     v *John*, b. March 23, 1749.

7. Elijah Bisbee[4] was chosen highway surveyor of
Pembroke in 1725 and constable in 1730. He had previously been mentioned in the records as a resident of that
town. There is no account of his marriage, though it is
well authenticated that he was married and had a family.
The following persons whose names appear on Pembroke
records, are doubtless his children:

13. i *Gideon*, b. —— ——; m. Rebecca Turner, Sept. 7, 1742.

---

* The following inscription is on her headstone in the old cemetery in Pembroke: "Here lies ye body of Mrs. Mary Bisbee, wife to Elisha Bisbee of Hingham, Gentleman, died April 16, 1737, in ye 82 year of her age."

† The records of Pembroke make the name of John Bisbee Jr.'s wife Rebecca
——, but records of Marshfield say he married Mary Oldham in 1710–11. He
may have had two wives. Pembroke records make Rebecca mother of the
above children.

14. ii *Elijah, Jr.*, b. ——, 1720 ; m. Deborah Sampson at Plympton, April 26, 1744.

iii *Sarah*, b. —— —— ; m. Amos Ford, Aug. 2, 1745.

iv *Mary*, b. —— —— ; m. Mathew Whiton, May 1, 1746.

8. Moses Bisbee[4] moved to East Bridgewater, where by wife Mary ——, had the following children :

i *Abigail*, d. young.

ii *Miriam*, b, 1724.

15. iii *Charles*, b. 1726 ; m. Beulah Howland.

iv *Joanna*, b. 1729 ; m. John Churchill.

v *Mary*, b. 1733 ; d. young.

vi *Tabitha*, b. 1735.

9. Elisha Bisbee[4] m. Patience Soanes at Pembroke, March 15, 1721–2.   Children :

16. i *Ebenezer*, b. Feb. 10, 1722.

ii *Martha*, b. Dec. 4, 1724 ; m. Thomas Standish, Jr., May 1, 1746.

iii *Betty*, b. Nov. 27, 1728.

17. iv *Elisha*, b. Aug. 22, 1731 ; m. Rebecca‿ ——.

v *Seth*, b. Feb. 5, 1736.

vi *Luther*, b. Dec. 7, 1738.

vii *Calvin*,   "   "

viii *Hannah*,* b. —— —— ; m. Zachariah Shaw, 1755.

18. ix *John*,* b. April 15, 1747.

10. Aaron Bisbee[4] m. Abigail ——, and had the following children, which are recorded in Pembroke :

i *Abigail*, b. June 16, 1721.

ii *Sarah*, b. Oct. 26, 1722 ; m.

19. iii *Aaron*, b. Aug. 20, 1724 ; m. Sarah Soule.

iv *Jemima*, b. May 14, 1726.

v *Rebecca*, b. May 18, 1741.

---

* These two names are not recorded on Pembroke records, and they are placed here on the authority of Mrs. Brown, daughter of the latter.

11. Hopestill Bisbee[4] was married to Hannah, daughter of William and Ruth Churchill of Plympton, Nov. 25, 1731, by Rev. Isaac Cushman. He died March 17, 1784, and his wife died Nov. 5, 1797, aged 90 years. Children :

    20. i *Abner*, b. June 16, 1739.
    21. ii *Hopestill*, b. May 28, 1741.
    22. iii *Esecher*, b. April 11, 1744.
         iv *Sary*, March 7, 1746–7.
         v *Hannah*, b. Feb. 20, 1751–2.

12. Elisha Bisbee[4] son of Elisha[3] of Hingham, is called "Esquire" in all the old records, and was much respected in Pembroke where he practiced the profession of law, and was known as the "Honest Lawyer." He was a member of the General Court from Pembroke, from 1725 to 1737, and died while a member of that body.* Sarah, widow of Elisha Bisbee, Esq., married for second husband Josiah Williams of Bridgewater, who was the father of Seth Williams and grandfather of the late Reuel Williams of Augusta. Children :

         i *Elisha*, b. —— ——; d. Aug. 20, 1723.
    23* ii *Samuel*, b. —— ——; m. Martha Snell, 1751.
         iii *Benjamin*, b. —— ——; killed in battle at the foot of
    Lake George, Sept. 8, 1755.

13. Gideon Bisbee[5] by wife Rebecca (Turner) had the following children, whose births are recorded in Pembroke:

         i *Lydia*, b. Sept. 21, 1744; d. young.
         ii *Lydia*, b. Feb. 19, 1746; m. Jos. Nichols July 11, 1772.
         iii *Jotham*, b. March 18, 1750.

---

* The following is inscribed on his headstone in the burying-ground at Pembroke : "Here lies ye body of Elisha Bisbee, Esq., aged 49 years, 12 days; died March ye 13, 1737."

iv *Rebecca*, b. March 16, 1752.

v *Gideon*, b. July 27, 1755.

vi *Jonathan*, b. Oct. 7, 1757.

14. Elijah Bisbee, Jr.,[5] m. Deborah Sampson of Plympton, April 26, 1744. She was the daughter of George Sampson and grandaughter of George Sampson. Elijah Bisbee died Sept. 28, 1804, aged 84 1-2 years. His wife Deborah died Oct. 25, 1815, aged 90 years and 7 months. Children :

    i *Hannah*, b. July 19, 1744 ; m. Job Weston.

24. ii *Elijah*, b. Sept. 4, 1746 ; m. Susannah Ripley.

25. iii *George*, b. Sept. 28, 1748 ; m. Grace Ripley.

26. iv *Noah*, b. May 23, 1752 ; m. Jenny Bradford.

27. v *John*, b. Sept. 15, 1755 ; m. Lydia Soule.

    vi *Asaph*, b. March 31, 1758 ; m. —— Douglass, lived in Carver.

    vii *Deborah*, b. Apr. 26, 1763 ; m. Josiah Perkins March 9, 1795.

    viii *Olive*, b. Dec. 5, 1769 ; d. March 10, 1832 ; unmarried.

15. Charles Bisbee[5] married Beulah Howland and moved to Sumner, Me., as previously stated. Children :

28. i *Elisha*, b. ——, 1757 ; m. Mary Pettingill, Duxbury, 1779.

29. ii *Charles*, b. —— 1758 ; m. Desire Dingley of Marshfield.

30. iii *Mary*, b. ——, 1760 ; m. Charles Ford.

31. iv *Moses*, b. Feb. 21, 1765 ; m. Ellen Buck.

32. v *John*, b. —— —— ; m. Sarah Philbrick.

33. vi *Solomon*, b. Sept. 3, 1769 ; m. Ruth Barrett.

34. vii *Calvin*, b. Oct. 14, 1771 ; m. Bethiah Glover.

35. viii *Rouse*, b. Oct. 17, 1775 ; m. Hannah Carrell.

36. ix *Celia*, b. —— ——; m. Joshua Ford.

16. Ebenezer Bisbee[5] m. 1st, Bathsheba Whitmarch, 1745 ; 2d, Mehitable, daughter of John Shaw. By first wife, who died 1777, he had, i *Jennet*, b. 1771, and probably others. He and his brother Luther moved to Plainfield.*

17. Elisha Bisbee, Jr.[5] married Rebecca ——, and had at Pembroke,

     i *Bethiah*, b. March 2, 1752.

18. John Bisbee[5] married first Rebecca, widow of Isaac Alden, in 1771; second, Huldah, daughter of Ebenezer Shaw, 1779; third, Mary, daughter of John Edson. He was a man of marked ability, and carried on business of various kinds. He owned a tannery, blacksmith shop, and was a large manufacturer of bricks; was also a farmer. He died in 1817. Children by first marriage:

     i *John*, b. 1774; removed to Maine.
     ii *Rebecca*, b. 1777.

By second marriage:

     iii *Ira*, b. —— 1780 ; m. Rebecca Dyke, 1805.
     iv *Ebenezer*, b. —— 1782 ; moved to Maine and m. there.
     v *Huldah*, b 1784; m. Wm. Barrell, Jr.; moved to Maine.
37. vi *Patty*, b. —— 1778 ; m. Dr. Benjamin Bradford.

By third wife :

38. vii *Asa*, b. June 15, 1789; moved to No. Yarmouth, Me.
     viii *Ziba*, b. March 17, 1792; m. Sirena Lincoln.
     ix *Olive*, b. Oct. 7, 1793; m. Cyrus Warren.
     x *Chandler*, b. Aug. 15, 1796; m Mary Whitmarsh.
     xi *Molly*, b. Feb. 21, 1798 ; m. Emery Brown.
     xii *Darius*, b. Apr. 19, 1799 ; went to Wisconsin.
39. xiii *Franklin*, b. May 26, 1800 ; m. Lovina Bisbee.
     xiv *Phedyma*, b. Jan. 2, 1802 ; d. Nov. 29, 1825.
     xv *Jefferson*, b. Apr. 30, 1803 ; m. Hannah Bisbee.
     xvi *Albert*, b. Dec. 19, 1804 ; m. Mary S. Endicott.

---

* Mitchell's History of Bridgewater.

xvii *Sylvia*, b. Sept. 8, 1806 ; m. 1st, Samuel Hollis ; 2d, Josiah Packard.

xviii *Almira*, b. May 8, 1809 ; m. Charles Simonds.

xix *Jndith*, b. Oct. 22, 1840 ; m. Levi Osborne.

19. Aaron Bisbee, Jr.,[5] married Sarah Soule of Duxbury, Nov. 26, 1747 ; lived in Duxbury.   Children :

  i *Joanna*, b. ——..

  ii *Abigail*, b. ——.

  iii *Studley*, b. ——, 1756; d. 1771.

  iv *Thomas*, b. ——, 1760; d. 1761.

  40. v *Oliver*, b. June 10, 1760; m. 1st, Huldah Simmons; 2d, Persis Simmons.

20. Abner Bisbee[5] married Bathsheba, b Jan. 12, 1735, daughter of Samuel Palmer of Halifax, Mass., formerly of Scituate.   He lived in Plympton and Rochester and died March 23, 1823.   His wife died Jan. 7, 1822. Children: · ·

  i *Lucy*, b. May 20, 1758; m. Ebenezer Cushman, Sept. 18, 1788.

  ii *Isaac*, b. Jan. 12, 1760.

  iii *Huldah*, b. Oct. 8, 1761; m. John Bartlett.

  iv *Ezra*, b. Oct. 8, 1763.

  v *Bathsheba*, b. Jan. 5, 1766; m. Samuel Bonney, Oct. 24, 1789.

  vi *Linda*, b. Aug. 22, 1768,

  vii *Abner*, b. July 24, 1771; m. Rebecca Churchill, Dec. 4, 1797.

  viii *Sarah*, b. March 1, 1774; m. John Morse, Middleboro'.

  ix *Betty*, b. Aug. 8, 1776; m. Zadoc Churchill.

21. Hopestill Bisbee, Jr ,[5] was married to Abigail, daughter of Nathaniel Churchill of Plympton, Sept. 4, 1766, by Rev. Jonathan Parker.   In 1771 he moved to Rochester where children were born of whom our record is

2

imperfect.   The two oldest were born in Plympton, the others in Rochester :

>   i *Abigail*, b. Oct. 21, 1768; m. Jonathan Hall.
>   ii *Hopestill*, b. Oct. 11, 1769; moved to Middleboro'.
>   iii *Sylvanus*, b. ——, 1783; d. April 23, 1812.
>   iv *Josiah*, b. —— ——; never married.
>   v *Ansel*, b. —— ——; moved to Buckfield, Me.; left no family.
>   vi *Levi*, b. —— ——.
>   vii *Susannah*, b. —— ——.
> viii *Hannah*, b. —— ——.

22.   Isecher Bisbee[5] was married to Mary, daughter of Thomas Harlow, by Rev. Jonathan Parker, Apr. 28, 1766. Children :

>   i *Molly*, b; Nov. 24, 1766.   m. Samuel ——
>   ii *Chloe*, b. Nov. 17, 1768.
>   iii *Isecher*, b. Aug. 21, 1771; m. Olive Barrows, Nov. 11, 1793.
>   iv *Hannah*, b. Apr. 2, 1774; m. Caleb Coombs.
>   v *Lois*, b. Apr. 7, 1777.
>   vi *Ephraim W.*, b. Aug. 28, 1779.
>   vii *Eunice*, b. June 6, 1782.
> viii *Patience*, b. June 28, 1785.
>   ix *Ira*, b. Feb. 11, 1788.
>   x *Deliverance Rouse*, b. Jan. 12, 1791.

23.   Samuel Bisbee[5] married Martha Snell and settled in Bridgewater A. D. 1750;   died in Stoughton in 1800. Children :

>   i *Sarah*, b. ——, 1751.
>   ii *Martha*, b. ——, 1753.
>   iii *Hannah*, b. ——, 1755.
>   iv *Samuel*, b. ——, 1757; m. Jerusha Pope.
> 41.   v *Benjamin*, b. ——, 1759; m. Milly Vose.
>   vi *Elisha*, b. —— ——; d. unmarried.
>   vii *Jonathan*, b. —— ——; m. Sarah Payson.

viii *Lovina*, b. —— ——; m. Alfred Howard.
ix *Mary*, b· —— ——.

24. Elijah Bisbee, Jr., Esq.,[6] married Susannah Ripley Dec. 16, 1773. He was town clerk of Plympton 16 years, an officer in the militia, an assessor, collector and treasurer of Plympton, and was much employed in public business; was appointed Justice of the Peace in 1793; represented the town in the legislature for 7 years, from 1808 to 1815, inclusive; by his mother he was a descendent of Myles Standish in the 6th degree. He died April 21, 1831. Susannah, his wife, died April 19, 1837, aged 91 years, 5 months and 19 days. Children:

 i *Elijah*, b. July 10, 1774; d. Nov. 23, 1797.
 ii *William*, b. Oct. 17, 1775; d. May 13, 1831, unmarried.
 iii *Susannah*, b. March 22, 1777; m. Polycarpus Parker.
42. iv *Bezai*, b. March 28, 1779; m. Betsey Marshal.
 v *Hannah*, b. Jan. 15, 1781; never married.
 vi *Infant*, b. June 27, 1784.
 vii *Polly*, b. July 3, 1785; m. Joseph Nye, 1814.
 viii *Zenas*, b. Apr. 3, 1787; d. May 8, 1788.

25. George Bisbee[6] married Grace, b. Oct. 26, 1753, daughter of William Ripley, Jr. The father died at Kingston March 2, 1839, aged 90 yrs. Grace, his wife, died Feb. 3, 1850, aged 96 years, 3 months and 7 days. Children :

 i *George*, b. March 1, 1774.
 ii *Daniel*, b. Jan. 19, 1776; m. Abigail Standish, Oct. 31, 1802.
 iii *Zebulon*, b. Feb. 9, 1778; m. Hannah Doten, Dec. 16, 1804.
 iv *Grace*, b. June 14, 1780.
 v *Asaph*, b. Dec. 5, 1784.
 vi *John*, b. Feb. 12, 1787.
 vii *Deborah*, b. Dec. 7, 1789.

viii *Lydia*, b. Feb. 23, 1792.
ix *Isaac*, b. July 20, 1794; d. unmarried.
x *Polly*, b. Dec. 6, 1798; m. Howard Chandler of Duxbury.

26.   Noah Bisbee[6] was married to Jenny Bradford, daughter of Gideon Bradford, Esq., Feb. 12, 1778. This family moved to Richmond, N. H., in April, 1806, where the mother died March 6, 1836, aged 82 years. The father died in January, 1839. Children:

    i *Jane*, b. Feb. 27, 1779.
    ii *Noah*, b. Feb. 17, 1781.*
    iii *Job*, b. Nov. 24, 1783.
    iv *Betsey*, b. Apr. 1, 1787.
    v *Seth*, b. June 11, 1779.
    vi *Sally*, b. Jan. 24, 1792.

27.   John Bisbee[6] was married to Lydia, b. Nov. 13, 1760, daughter of Ephraim Soule, Nov. 13, 1791, by Rev. Ezra Sampson. He died June 24, 1842; he was a revolutionary pensioner. His wife died Oct. 13, 1826. Children:

    i *Infant*, b. Dec. 30, 1792; d. Jan. 4, 1793.
43. ii *John*, b. May 12, 1794; m.
    iii *Zenas*, b. Feb. 10, 1796; d. Feb. 3, 1817.
    iv *Lydia S.*, b. Apr. 18, 1799; d. May 6, 1825.
    v *Rebecca*, b. March 28, 1803.

28.   Elisha Bisbee,[6] oldest child of Charles Bisbee,[5] was married in Duxbury, Mass., in 1779, to Mary Pettingill of that town. He came to Sumner with the rest of the family, where his children, all except the two oldest, were

---

* Killed in battle at Bridgewater, in Upper Canada, July 24, 1814, (war of 1812). He left a son, Wm. Bradford Bisbee, b. Dec. 22, 1811.

born. We have no record of his death, or of that of his wife. Children:

i *Susan*[7] b. March 26, 1780, m. to Nathaniel Bartlett of Hartford, March 28, 1802, and had America, b. Apr. 18, 1803, m. Lydia Hayford May 31, 1830 ; Lamira, b. Apr. 17, 1804, m. Oliver Lawrence, d. Dec. 26, 1872, at Wayne ; Fidelia, b. Sept. 11, 1805, m. Zeri Hayford ; Hiram, b. Nov. 1, 1811, d. May 13, 1839, without issue ; Sarah H., b. Sept. 29, 1814, m. Dennis Kilbreth, d. April 19, 1861 ; Horatio, b. Nov. 2, 1816, d. Apr. 23, 1842, without issue ; Susan B., b. Feb. 13, 1819, d. Oct. 11, 1841.

ii *Sally*[7] b.——; m. Gad Hayford of Hartford. Children : Charles, Axel, Harrison, Cyrus m. Arvilla Bartlett, and Asia. (Most of these had families but we have no record.)

iii *Anna*[7] b.——; m. March 24, 1805, to Stephen Drew of Turner, by Rev. Thomas Macomber. Children :

(1) Arvilla, b. June 7, 1806, m. Martin Harris, 2d, of Turner, and had Albion, b. Nov. 2, 1830, d. Dec. 2. 1834 ; William W., b. Apr. 28, 1833, m. Hannah Robbins ; Stephen D., b. March 25, 1835, m. Flora Harlow ; Angelia, b. Aug. 22, 1839, m. Luther Tripp.

(2) Phidella, b. June 7, 1806, m. Asa Coburn of Turner, Dec. 24, 1826, and had Jesse D., b. May 2, 1828 ; Asa, b. Apr. 26, 1833 ; Mary A., b. Jan. 17, 1836 ; Greenlief H., b. March 7, 1839.

(3) Jesse, b. Sept. 21, 1808, m. 1st in May 1834 to Hannah T. Phillips of Turner, and had Hannah Gorham, b. July 27, 1835 d. June 23, 1842 ; Franklin Mellen* b. July 19, 1837, m. Araminta Blanche Woodman of Naples, had a son which died young; Delphina M., b. Nov. 24, 1839, d. Dec. 22, 1861 ; Anna P., b. Jan. 8, 1842, m. Robert H. Perkins, July 23, 1864 ; George E., b. Feb. 13, 1845, m. March 3, 1869, to Edna Flint. For second wife Jesse Drew, m. Dec. 14, 1857, Clara Wellington, and had Gertrude H., b. July 21, 1859 ; Morrill N., b. May 17, 1862. Mrs. Drew d. Oct. 27, 1867.

---

* He is a graduate of Bowdoin College, and by profession a lawyer. He has been clerk and assistant clerk of the Maine House of Representatives; was Capt, Major and Brevet Col. of the 15th Maine Regiment in the war of the Rebellion; served four years as Secretary of State, and has been twice appointed Pension Agent, which office he now holds; resides in Augusta.

(4) Louisa, b. Nov. 23, 1810, m to Nehemiah B. Bicknell of Turner, Me., by Rev. Seth Stetson, Dec. 24, 1832, and had William Otis, b. March 12, 1834, d. Dec. 12, 1862 ; Albion Harris, b. Mar. 18, 1836, m. July 20, 1875, by Rev. Charles M. Smith to Margaret E. Peabody. Mrs. Bicknell the mother, died Aug. 2, 1846.

(5) Molly, b. Apr. 20, 1813, d. June 18, 1851.

iv *Elisha* Jr.,[7] b. May 8, 1786, m. to Joanna Sturtevant of Sumner, by Isaac Sturtevant, Esq., Apr. 10, 1810. Thomas J. Bisbee d. Dec. 10, 1874. Children :

(1) Elbridge G., b. Feb. 8, 1811, d. Oct. 2, 1812.

(2) Thomas J., b. July 6, 1812, m. in June, 1840, to Sylvia Stevens of Rumford, and had Mary A., b. June —, 1840 ; Augusta, b. 1843, m. in 1862 to a Putnam of Rumford. He died Feb. 6, 1875.

(3) George W., b. July 6, 1812, m. Jan. 1, 1836, to Mary B. Howe of Rumford, and had George Dana*, b. July 9, 1841, who was married to Anna Louise Stanley, July 8, 1866, and has had four children, two of whom survive. Geo. W. Bisbee died in Peru, Me., Jan. 27, 1872.

(4) Mary P., b. June 6, 1815, m. Freeman Reed of Hartford, Apr. 1, 1840, and had Augustus, b. Apr. 13, 1842, m. Mary Tyler ; Joanna B., b. Dec. 12, 1844, m. Oscar Hayford ; Jane E., b Sept. 23, 1846, m. Edwin Bettinson ; Mary B., b. June 26, 1849, m. Frank Fowler ; Elisha B., b. Jan. 20, 1853.

(5) Elisha S., b. Apr., 1822, d. Sept. 24, 1823.

Elisha, Jr., married for second wife May 9, 1825, Fanny Bryant. Children :

(6) Sabra W., b., Feb. 21, 1826, m. Orville Robinson of Hartford, Apr. 14, 1845, and had Fanny B., b. 1845, m. Llewellyn Heald, and Henry R., b. 1854.

(7) Sophia G., b. April 7, 1827.

(8) Levi B., b. July 10, 1828, m. Eliza A. S. Heald, and had Minnie, Harvey and others.

(9) Elisha S., b. Apr. 15, 1830, m. Jan. 4, 1857, to Jane Parsons of Hartford, and had Leetta, Harriet and Hiram.

(10) Asia H., b. Jan. 6, 1832, m. and d. at Portland, Oregon, June 1, 1870, leaving two children.

---

* He was an officer in the 16th Maine Regiment and is now an Attorney at Law in Buckfield, Me., and Attorney for the county.

(11) Daniel H., b. Oct. 9, 1833 ; never married.

(12) Jane Y., b. July 1, 1835, m. James McDonald Oct. 1, 1855.

(13) Hopestill R., b. June 21, 1837, m. to Ella —— Sept. 14, 1872, at Virginia City, Nevada, and had Daniel, b. Sept, 1872, and Hopestill b. July, 1874.

(14) Hiram R., b. Dec. 11, 1839. Shot dead at Bermuda Hundred, Va , May 20, 1864. Sergt. in Co. F. 9th Me. Vols.

v *Daniel*, b. ——, ——; m. Sylvia Stevens of Sumner. Our records of this family are very incomplete. Children :

(1) William S., b. June 4, 1817, m. Aug. 23, 1838, Emeline Spaulding of Sumner, d. Sept. 10, 1865. Had Francis M., who m. Apr. 29, 1867, Ella C. Heald of Sumner.

(2) Danville b. ——, ——; m. Martha A. Robinson of Sumner, and had two daughters, viz.: Mary E. m. a Briggs, and M. Anna m. a Richardson and resides in Medford, Mass. Daniel Bisbee died and his widow married a Pomeroy and resides at East Sumner.

(3) Ezra S., b. ——, ——; m. Margaret Spaulding of Buckfield.

(4) Sylvia S., b. Nov. 13, 1824, m. to Robert E. Stewartson, a native of England, Oct. 24, 1846, by Vernon Stiles, Esq., and had Addie E.; b. Apr. 12, 1850, d. Apr. 13, 1850 ; Eugene A., b. Aug. 27, 1852, d. Oct. 23, 1853 ; Lilligene L., b. Jan. 3, 1854 ; Jennie L., b. June 18, 1856, d. June 9, 1865 ; Willie E., b. Aug. 13, 1858 ; Ida E., Inez E., (twins) b. June 14, 1861, both d. young ; Sylvia E., b. Dec. 19, 1863 ; Lottie D., b. Jan. 22, 1865; resides in West Medway, Mass.

vi *Hopestill* was b. Apr. 27, 1796 in Sumner, and was m. Dec. 18, 1817, to Martha Sturtevant of the same town, by Isaac Sturtevant, Esq. Children :

(1) Deplura, b. July 11, 1818, m. in Jan. 1846, to Lydia B. Heald of Sumner, and had Alfaretta, b. Dec. 2, 1847, d. March 24, 1852 ; Columbus H., b. Dec. 20, 1844, d. Oct. 2, 1872 ; Fred W., b. Sept. 2, 1856 ; W. Frank, b. June 17, 1858. This family resides in Camden, Me.

(2) Lavinia B., b. Sept. 10, 1820, m. Sept. 18, 1844, to Stephen R. Robinson of Sumner, and has Horatio N., b. Aug. 9, 1845.

(3) Horatio M. b. Nov. 2, 1822, d. Dec. 22, 1844.

(4) Martha J., b. Apr. 4, 1828, m. to M. Chauncey Osgood of Hartford, Nov. 29, 1852, and had Merrick H , b. Feb. 15, 1857, Cleon S., b. July 22, 1859.

(5) Henrietta B., b. June 26, 1838, m. 1st to Geo. C. Thompson Feb. 14, 1856, who d. Aug. 17, 1863; m. 2d Samuel H. Maxim of Peru, and had Hannah, b. July 20, 1866 ; H. Welma, b. Apr. 10, 1869.

vii *Molly*, b. Jan. 4, 1794, was m. first to Nehemiah Bryant and had :

(1) Hannibal B., b. Jan. 12, 1811, m. May 19, 1833, to Betsey B. Stetson, and 2d to Mary A. Ross of Turner, Oct. 16, 1854. His children by first wife were Lewis C., b. June 7, 1834, m. Martha Staples ; Mary Ann, b. Nov. 20, 1836, m. Charles Pratt ; Huldah R., b. Dec. 25, 1838, m. William Harlow ; Elisha S., b. Feb. 14, 1841, killed in the army May 23, 1864, at North Anna river ; Hannibal, b. Dec. 9, 1842, m. Lucy A. Bicknell ; William H. b. July 16, 1846 ; Roland E., b. May 22, 1849, d. Apr. 23, 1850 ; Betsey S., b. Feb. 1, 1852, m. Wm. A. Haney. By second wife, Russell Everett, b. May 14, 1856 ; Dennis, b. Oct. 1, 1857 ; Martha H., b. June 16, 1859.

(2) Phebe B., d. young.

(3) Horatio B., d. young.

(4) Anne D., b. May 20, 1819, m. June 17, 1838, to John J. Glover.

For second husband, Molly (Bisbee) Bryant was married Oct. 3, 1825, to Lemuel Dunham of Hartford, by Rev. Daniel Hutchinson. Children :

(5) Mary B., b. March 26, 1826, m. to Allen J. Sturtevant, d. July 5, 1848.

(6) Phebe, b. May 26, 1827, m. Oct. 7, 1849, to Moses Alley of Hartford, and had Adelbert H., b. July 16, 1850, m. Oct. 17, 1875 ; to Mary E. Sampson ; Mary A., b. Jan. 5, 1852 ; Ida C., b. Sept. 14, 1853, m. Nov. 8, 1874, to Benj. F. Glover ; Martha F., b. Aug. 4, 1855 ; Flora May, b. July 15, 1858 ; Herbert L., b. June 29, 1860 ; Arthur M., b. July 27, 1863 ; Phebe E., b. July 17, 1866 ; Gertie C., b. May 23, 1868 ; Everet V., b. Feb. 14, 1871.

(7) Amanda, b. Dec. 10, 1828, m. April 30, 1848, to James Gammon, d. Sept. 30, 1850

(8) Lemuel, b. Aug. 26, 1830, m. Jan. 1, 1859, to widow Lydia A. (Cummings) Clifford of Woodstock, and had Jabez W., b. Oct. 1859, d. Jan. 1862 ; Carrie E., b. Feb. 25, 1863 ; Elvira B., b. Sept.

9, 1873. He resides at Bryant's Pond, Me. Lemuel Dunham, the second husband of Molly Bisbee, for second wife married Tabitha Briggs of Woodstock, Me., who survived him and married a Coffin of Albany.

  viii *Thersea*, b. ——, ——; m. Barney Howard, and had :
  (1) Angeline, b. ——, ——; never married.
  (2) Edwin. b. ——, ——; m. Harriet Barrell.
  (3) Asia, b. ——, ——; m. ——, ——.
  (4) Adoniram, b. ——, ——; m. ——, ——.
  (5) Maria A., b. ——, ——; m. ——, ——.

  ix *Huldah*, b. 1803 ——; m. Sampson Reed of Hartford, and d. in 1842. Children :
  (1) Elisha, b. ——, ——; m. Emma Brett of Canton, d. 1851.
  (2) Emily, b. ——, ——; m. Lewis Childs.
  (3) Lewis, b. ——, ——; m. Salome Barrell of Hartford.
  (4) Sampson, b. ——, ——; m. Adrian Marble, Dixfield.
  (5) Huldah, b. ——, ——; m. Bradbury Richardson.
  (6) Lydia, b. ——, ——; m. Joseph Richardson.
  (7) Axel, b. ——, ——; m. ——, ——; went to Minnesota.
  (8) Augustus, b. ——, ——; d. ——, ——.

  x *Horatio*, b. Aug. 13, 1800, m. Eunice White of Sumner, March 27, 1823. Children :

  (1) Esther H., b. Oct. 29, 1823, m. Elbridge Gammon of Hartford, July 4, 1834, by Benj. Dearborn, Esq., and had Roscoe, b. March, 1843, m. Clara Reynolds, and Thomas W., b. Feb. 1851, m. Estella Varney.

  (2) Daniel, b. Jan. 25, 1826, m. Philindia F. Lombard of Turner, June 6, 1847, by Rev. A. Wheeler, and had Charles M., b. Nov. 21, 1848, m. Ella R. Tucker, Aug. 6, 1871 ; Huldah L., b. Dec. 7, 1850, m. Sept. 18, 1870, Reuel G. Jackson ; George E. b. Aug. 30, 1853, m. Anna M. Jones ; Edward L., b. Nov. 6, 1860 ; Elisha F., b. Sept. 27, 1862.

  (3) Elizabeth H., b. Sept. 25, 1828, m. Thomas C. Gammon of Canton, Dec. 31, 1847, by Benj. Dearborn, Esq., and had Fairfield J., b. Nov. 4, 1848, m. Jane Hall, Jan. 31, 1869 ; George J., b. June 6, 1850, m. Betsey Lombard, Jan. 1, 1870 ; Alfred T., b. Apr. 28,

1852 ; Sylvester, b. Nov. 17, 1853 ; Arthur H., b. Nov. 18, 1856, and Florilla E., b. Jan. 7, 1859.

(4) Susan, b. Apr. 25, 1829, m. to Robert P. Briggs of Auburn, March 20, 1853, by Cyrus Thompson, Esq., and had Walter S., b. March 12, 1854 ; Otis H., b. Sept. 30, 1858 ; John II., b. July 5, 1863 ; Fred A., b. Aug. 29, 1866.

(5) Dolly K., b. Feb. 4, 1831, m. Daniel W. Tyler of China, Me., Sept. 11, 1853, and had William T., b. July 21, 1854 ; John L., b. Jan. 25, 1858. This family resides in Gardiner, Me.

(6) Abbie F., b. Apr. 4, 1833, m. May 16, 1852, to William A. Goddard of Augusta, Me., and had Julia M. b. Apr. 9, 1853, m. I. S. Reynolds ; Abbie E., b. May 23, 1859. This family resides at Week's Mills, China.

(7) Eunice W., b. Jan. 12, 1837, m. March 5, 1854, to Samuel P. Merrill of Andover, Me., and had Matilda A., b. Dec. 3, 1854, d. Apr. 19, 1875 ; Lizzie M., b. July 27, 1856 ; George H., b. Dec. 7, 1857.

(8) Horatio, Jr., b. May 1, 1839, was Lt. Col. of the 9th Me. Vols.; after the war was over he moved to Florida and was made U. S. District Attorney. He was married Apr. 5, 1863, but we have no record of his family.

(9) Elisha, b. Feb. 11, 1843, was a member of Co. F. 9th Me. Vols., and died at Hilton Head, Jan. 4, 1862.

(10) Hannah M., b. June 13, 1847.

29. Charles Bisbee, Jr., was born in 1757, and was married to Desire Dingley of Marshfield. He was a jeweller and watch repairer and worked some time at his trade in Brunswick, Me. He subsequently moved with his family to Indiana, where he died June 11, 1833. I have not been furnished with the dates of birth of his children, most of whom are dead. His grandchildren reside in the West. Children :

i *Isaiah*, b. ——, ——, d. 1833.

ii *Mary*, b. ——, ——, m. Dent, d. Sept. 20, 1822.

iii *Susan*, b. ——, ——, m. Stockum ; d. Oct. 1833.

iv *Desire*, b. ——, ——-, m. Egelston, d. June 29, 1855.

v *Charles*, Jr., b. ——, ——; d. June, 1856.

vi *Ezra*, b, ——, —— , d. 1862,

vii *John*, b. ——, ——-, d. May 5, 1875.

viii *Harriet*, b. Aug. 31, 1800, m. to Henry Walker of Dearborn Co , Ind., by Judge John Livingston, Dec. 11, 1822. She resides at Aurora, Ind., and her husband or son is Postmaster there. Their children are Frances, born Aug. 24, 1824, d. Aug. 29, 1833 ; John, born Aug. 18, 1826, married Jan. 18, 1848, to Rachel Chisman.

30. Mary Bisbee,[6] b. Apr. 28, 1760, was married to Charles Ford of Pembroke, Mass., afterwards of Sumner. Children :

i *Seth*, b. Dec. 25, 1781 in Pembroke, m. Sally Nason, and had :
(1) Mary B., b. Apr. 12, 1806.
(2) Elhanan W., b. Nov. 20, 1807.
(3) Susan M., b. July 10, 1809.
(4) Minerva J., b. Sept 8, 1811.
(5) Maxlana A., b. June 8, 1813.
(6) Lucy M., b. April 18, 1815.
(7) Benjamin F., b. March 31, 1817.
(8) George W., b. Nov. 24, 1819.
(9) Rosanna W., b. March 24. 1821.
(10) Angeline M., b. Jan. 23, 1825.
(11) Columbus F., b. Apr. 1, 1828.

ii *Charles**, Jr., b. Apr. 8, 1784, m, Rebecca Fletcher, and had
(1) Timothy, b. 1807.
(2) Charles A., b. Dec. 20, 1810, m. Nov. 1835, Eliza A. C. Hapgood, resides at South Waterford, and his children are Charles H., b. June 8, 1836 ; Acelia E., b. Nov. 25, 1837 ; Oscar R., b. June 22, 1840 ; Ella F., b. May 30, 1843 ; Ada A., b. Sept. 29, 1846.

---

* It states on his grave stone in Sumner, that he was the first white child born in that town.

iii *Joshua*, b. Nov. 9, 1785, d. an infant.

iv *Mary*, B., b.——,——; d. unmarried, aged 18 years.

31. Moses Bisbee was married October 14, 1789, to Ellen Buck of New Gloucester, by Rev. John Strickland, minister of Turner. He resided many years in Bethel, at the middle of the town, called Middle Intervale. He was an ingenious blacksmith, and much of the table cutlery used in his time, in his vicinity, was made by him. He died in Waterford June 23, 1852, aged 86 years, 11 mos. Children :

i *Polly*, b. Sept. 21, 1790, m. Dec. 9, 1812, to Roswell Adley of Albany, Me., and had Hesediah, b. Nov. 2, 1813, m. Apr. 26, 1832, to George Clark ; Elvira, b. May 2, 1815, m. Aug. 17, 1852, to Charles Bisbee ; Harriet W., b. June 5, 1817, m. June 9, 1837, to Martin Sylvester ; Roswell, b. Feb. 15, 1819, m. 1847, to Joanna Black ; Warren M., b. Jan. 30, 1821, m. 1841 Hannah Smith ; Lafayette, b. Oct. 26, 1824, m. 1850, Lois L. Whittier, d. Nov. 18, 1862 ; Lydia M., b. March 15, 1826, d. Dec. 22, 1848 ; Persis E., b. June 19, 1829, m. Aug. 3, 1848 Milton F. Kimball ; Moses W., b. Oct. 25, 1832, m. June 15, 1868, Lucinda Munson.

ii *Moses*, Jr., b. June 1, 1792, m. first in 1814 Hannah, daughter of James and Hannah (Shattuck) Swan of Bethel, and had Elizabeth A., born Oct. 3, 1815, m. in 1842, to Daniel Hollinger, d. June 13, 1844 ; Calvin, b. 1817, went to sea and has not since been heard from ; Charles D., b. Aug. 24, 1822, m. March 1, 1847, Maria M. Long ; Leander D., b. May 1, 1824, m. April 11, 1854, Sarah E. Day ; Alpheus S., b. Apr. 15, 1826, m. Dec. 5, 1850, Mary A. Day ; William W., b. 1828, was a soldier in the Mexican War, and died at Puebla, Mexico, Aug. 23, 1847 ; Sybil A., b. 1830, d. 1833.

For second wife, Moses Bisbee married Eleanor, daughter of James Beattie of Bethel, and had Algernon S., b. May 27, 1834, m. June 19, 1868, Angie Emery ; Hannah S., b. March 19, 1839, m. 1862, Nathaniel Stevens ; Albert P., b. Apr. 15, 1841, m. Keziah Adley, 1863.

iii *Robert D.*, b. Aug. 28, 1792, m. Ellen Foster of Bridgton, and had Lucinda, b.——, ——; d. in infancy ; Phebe F. b. Dec. 24, 1819, d. Sept. 5, 1844 ; Lydia L., b. May 7, 1822, m. 1847, Phineas Weymouth, d. Aug. 27, 1847 ; Robert b. Aug. 27, 1824, m. Elmira Kelley.

For second wife Robert D. Bisbee m. Mehitable M. Trott, and had Sarah A., b. June 25, 1829, d. Sept. 15, 1831 ; Zilphia, b. June 2, 1832, m. Nov. 27, 1852, A. A. Burnham.

iv *Calvin*, b. June 3, 1796, no further record.

v *Jonathan T.*, b. Nov. 4, 1799, d. Nov. 12, 1857.

vi *Ellen C.*, b. Apr. 16, 1801, m. Dennis Brackett of Bridgton, and had three children who died at Bridgton, names unknown ; Edward B., b. Jan. 23, 1826, d. Nov. 26, 1867; Susan ; George S ; Miranda ; Dennis ; Nathan C ; Lonsville W., killed July 21, 1861 at the battle of Bull Run ; Susan J.; Oliver B. and Charles W. Most of them died unmarried.

32. John Bisbee was married to Sarah Philbrick of Buckfield, April 1, 1792, by Ichabod Bonney, Esq. He was familiarly known as "Uncle Johnny Bisbee." He resided in Sumner; was a farmer and blacksmith, and a famous bear and fox hunter. He was eccentric, but withal a good citizen. The date of his death is not reported. Children :

i *Elizabeth*, b. Jan. 13, 1794, married to Asa Bonney of Hartford, on the 26th of Aug, 1810, by Isaac Sturdevant, and had Elmira, b. Feb. 4, 1810; Sarah, b. Nov. 11, 1812 ; Abigail, b. July 1, 1814 ; John, b. Nov. 8, 1815 ; Stephen, b. May 5, 1817 ; Ann, b. Sept. 3, 1818; Vesta, b. Nov. 23, 1819; Mary, b. Aug. 22, 1821; Elizabeth, b. Apr. 21, 1823, d./ Jan. 5, 1824; Elizabeth, b, 1824; Isaac, b. 1826; Asa, b. 1827; Lydia, b. 1829; Cyrus, b. 1830; Charles, b. 1832; James, b. 1834; Fanny, b. 1836; Thankful, b. 1839; eighteen in all.

ii *Celia*, b. Apr. 26, 1796; m. Martin Drake of Buckfield. Children: Dorcas, m. Stephen Gammon; Sarah J., m. Charles Dunn; Celia V., m. George Long; Achsa, m. John Dammon; Esther, m. Bradbury Dammon.

iii *John*, b. January, 1797; d. young.

iv *Eliab*, b. June 23, 1799; m. Melissa —— of Sumner, Me., June 6, 1819. Children: Arvilla S., b. Oct. 7, 1819; m. Bradley Keen, July 26, 1846; Asaniah D., b. Jan. 5, 1821; m. Bashaba Turner, Sept. 25, 1849; Welthea, b. March 27, 1823; m. Matthew Childs; Samira, b. Jan. 24, 1825, d. Sept. 7, 1842; Mara, b March 29, 1826; Annis P., b. Feb. 7, 1829, m. John Keen, Nov. 21, 1848; Eliab, b. Nov. 17, 1830, m. Theresa Dearborn; Cynthia H., b. July 29, 1833, m. Benjamin Chase, March 22, 1855; Melissa, b. Aug. 1835, d. June 12, 1860.

v *Dolly*, b. Feb. 18, 1801, m. Thaddeus Thompson of Hartford, March 6, 1823, and had Charles B., b Jan. 25, 1824, m. Jane Crosby, Nov. 17, 1848 ; George W., b. Aug. 10, 1826, m. Joanna Keen; Harriet M., b. May 20, 1828, m. Geo. W. Lee; Benj. F., b. Jan. 28, 1829, m. Abby Warner, July 2, 1854; Leander, b. ——, ——; John, b. May 13, 1840; Royal, b. Aug. 17, 1842; Mary E., b. March 11, 1844.

vi *Charles*, b. Nov. 18, 1803, m. Charlotte Weaver, who had George H. b. —— ——, m, Martha Hersey: Celia, b.—— ——; m. Cyrus Bishop of Peru; Charlotte, b. ——, ——; m. Seth Allen; Beulah, b. ——, ——; Mary, b. Dec. 26, 1828, m. Caleb Marston; Sarah, b. Dec. 11, 1833, m. Timothy Partridge; Andrew, b. ——, ——; Charles, Jr., b. ——, ——, m. Olive Frazier.

vii *Mary*, b. Sept. 2, 1804, married Samuel Rice of Waterford, and had Maria, b. Feb. 10, 1840, m. George ——; Harriet, b. Oct. 18, 1842; Sophia, b. Sept. 1844; Annette, b. Sept. 1846, d. March 18, 1847; Mary, b. July, 1848, m. —— Morse; Thomas, b. Apr. 1. 1850, m. Lucy Jewett.

viii *Desire*, b. Dec. 10, 1806, m. William Drake of Buckfield, afterwards of Paris, Aug. 26, 1827, and had George R., b. Jan. 13, 1829, m. Maria Austin, June, 1860; Desire B., b. Apr. 30, 1843, m. William Mooney of West Paris, Jan. 15, 1867

ix *Jones*, b Feb. 2, 1809, m. Rebecca Robinson of Sumner, June 6, 1838, and had John, b. Apr. 16, 1839, m. May, 23, 1863, Adelia Small; Abbie, b. Sept. 10, 1841, m. Fernando Allen, 1862, d. Mar. 20, 1873; Sylvester, b. Nov. 17, 1851.

x *Stephen*, b. March 2, 1810, married Velzora Russell of Hartford, in 1834. They had Belinda; Sarah; Jane, m. Lewis Leavitt;

Ephraim, m. Adelaide Frizell; William, m. Sarah Dunham; Lucy, m. Russell Pratt; Mary, m. Cyrus Glover; Elvira, m. John Elwell.

xi *Harriet*, b. Nov. 18, 1812, married to James Tyler of Peru, Apr. 27, 1831, by Dr. Bethuel Cony. Children: Gilbert, b. Feb. 5, 1832, m. July 4, 1860, Martha Linnell; Desire, b. July 14, 1834, m. Feb. 6, 1854, Andrew Abbott, d. Oct. 12, 1855; Mary E., b. Jan. 27, 1840, m. Apr. 14, 1864, Asa Jones; Harriet B., b. Apr. 4, 1844, m. Apr 5, 1867, Loring Hunton; Annette, b. June 13, 1847, d. Aug. 6. 1856.

33. We know very little of Solomon Bisbee, save that he was a farmer and resided in Sumner. He was married May 10, 1795, by Ichabod Bonney, Esq., to Ruth Barrett of Sumner. Children :

i *Luther*, b. March 11, 1796; m. Mary Wardwell of Albany, March 19, 1827, and had Hiram, b. Jan. 9, 1828; Maria, b. Jan. 2, 1831, d. Feb. 15, 1834; Addison, b. Jan. 4, 1834; Columbia, b. Sept. 16, 1836, m. Levi Millett Jan. 25, 1854; Caroline, b. Jan. 6, 1839, m. Francis M. Sampson Sept. 11, 1860; Byron, b. Oct. 22, 1841, m. Adaline Knight Oct. 3, 1865; Walter, b. Jan. 1, 1844; Winslow, b. Nov. 21, 1845; Infant son, b. May 1, 1849, d. May 23, 1849.

ii *Abel W.*, b. Feb. 6, 1798. He was Postmaster at Sumner 23 years; often held town office and member of the Legislature in 1850; m. June 1, 1828, Polly Record of Hebron; 2d, Apr. 8, 1832, to Nancy Durell of Woodstock. Children: George, b. —— 20, 1829; Polly, b. Feb. 8, 1835; Nancy, b. July 28, 1837; Antepast D., b. Dec. 3, 1840.

iii *Beulah*, b. Dec. 17, 1799; m. Joseph Benson of Paris, March 26. 1820. Children : Abel S., b. April 2, 1821; m. Deborah B. Phillips Oct. 22, 1848; Ruth B., b. June 19, 1822, m. Benj. Young, Jr., July 13, 1845; William W., b. Nov. 30, 1823, m. Mary A. P. Dunham Oct. 19, 1845; Fidelia, b. Apr. 7, 1825, m. Asia Keen July 27, 1845; Mary A., b. Feb. 17, 1827, m. Israel A. Fletcher May 25, 1845; Benjamin F., b. July 1, 1828, d. Dec. 11, 1828; Joseph F., b. Apr. 23, 1830, m. Sarah A. Ryerson May 9, 1858; America B., b. Oct. 21, 1831; Elbridge S., b. Apr. 28, 1833, m.

Jane L. Russell Dec. 18, 1858; Thomas H. B., b. May 30, 1835, m. Amanda F. Cushman Oct. 6, 1859; Sylvia H., b. Aug. 23, 1836, m. Decatur Monk March 29, 1857; Calvin B., b. Aug. 27, 1838, m. Rosabella Cushman Jan. 5, 1864; Sophia M., b. Sept. 27, 1840, m. John B. Hathaway; John M., b. Apr. 9, 1843, d. Oct. 24, 1862.

iv *Holland*, b. Dec. 15, 1801.

v *Ruth*, b. March 22, 1803, m. Clarendon Walker of Paris, Nov. 14, 1825. She died Sept. 6, 1839. Children: Lucy A., b. Dec. 18, 1827, m. John W. Allen, 1852; Solomon, b. July 2, 1829, d. 1833; Henry R. b. March 7, 1830, m. Adelia Mason, 1856; Maranda, b. May 27, 1833, m. George T. Bowker, May, 1854; Leander C., b. June 4, 1835, m. Sarah Thomas, May, 1860; Aurelia R., b. Apr. 25, 1837, m. Nelson R. Swift, Nov. 1856; Esther A., b. Apr. 1, 1839, m. Roscoe Tuell, May, 1862.

vi *Anna*, b. Dec. 25, 1806, m. Abel Fletcher of Sumner, Feb. 5, 1832, resides at West Sumner. Children: Harriet A., b. Sept 25, 1832, m. Luther Hollis; Rachel R. b. Jan 17, 1837, m. Addison G. Parlin, Nov. 21, 1866 ; Abel T., b. June 16, 1841, d. June 26, 1856.

vii *Solomon*, Jr. b. Dec. 2, 1808, married June 12, 1837, to Hannah P. Heald of Sumner. He resides in Sumner. Children: Timothy H., b. Sept. 2, 1838, m. Nov. 5, 1873, Julia Wright of Dallas City, Oregon; Maria, b. July 2, 1841, m. Sept. 18, 1869, O. P. Houghton Emporia, Kansas; George G., b. July 11, 1843, d. Aug. 13, 1845; Lewis H., b. June 9, 1850, m. June 9, 1870, to Eva R. Robbins.

viii *Esther S.*, b. Dec. 19, 1810, was married to James M. Gammon of Hartford, Me., Sept. 19, 1830, by Simeon Barrett, Esq., resides at East Sumner. Children: Fanny W., b. July 11, 1830, d. Oct. 19, 1865; Nathaniel, b. March 22, 1832, d. Sept. 24, 1854; Solomon B., b. Feb. 5, 1834, m. Cynthia E. Ames, March 17, 1874; Charles H., b. Sept. 27, 1835, m. Maria Barrows, Aug. 11, 1871; Ruth B., b. Aug. 13, 1838, m. Dec. 28, 1858, Samuel S. Crockett; Lydia B., b. Dec. 29, 1840, m. Jan. 22, 1859, Albion Hollis; William W. b. May 12, 1843, m. Nov. 16, 1869, to Eusebia N. Hines; Israel F., b. Jan. 16, 1847, m. July 15, 1872, Addie E. Glover; Abby S., b. Jan. 1847, d. Feb. 5, 1854; Horace, b. Nov. 30, 1850, m. March 15, 1874, to Sarah J. Russell; Anna F., b. Feb. 10, 1853, d. Apr. 12, 1854.

ix *America,* born Dec. 20, 1811, was by occupation a blacksmith at North Paris, now resides at Norway. He was first married to Olive Gurney of Hebron, in Sept. 1831, by Stephen Myrick Esq., 2d to Cynthia C., widow of Dr. Rowe of North Paris, Dec. 30, 1846, and 3d, to Clara Tuttle of Buckfield, Oct. 15, 1868. Children, both by first marriage: Miriam, b. Dec. 1, 1832, m. Nathan D. Libby of Lewiston, Me.; Wright, b. July 6, 1833, m. Georgie Lamb of Bennington, Vermont.

x *Jonas,* b. April 27, 1818, was married to Mary J. Walker of Danville, March 15, 1840, by Rev. W. F. Eaton. He resides at North Paris. Children: Ira W., b. Nov. 29, 1842, d. March 19, 1863; Mary J., b. Feb. 4, 1845, m. Charles E. Stephens Oct. 2, 1865; Calvin, b. March 17, 1847, m. Fanny Churchill Jan. 6, 1874; Esther A., b. March 18, 1849, m. Adna R. Tuell; William F., b. Aug. 19, 1855.

34. Calvin Bisbee lived and died on the old Bisbee Homestead in Sumner. He was much respected in town and often held town office. He was a member of the convention which framed the Constitution of the State, and subsequently served as a member of the Legislature. He was married Apr. 22, 1800, by Rev. Isaac Sturtivant, to Bethiah Glover of Buckfield. Children:

i *Volney,* b. July 3, 1810, was married Jan. 8, 1827, by Dr. Bethuel Cary, to Ruth Briggs of Hartford, and had Daniel, born Apr. 27, 1835.

ii *David,* b. Dec. 14, 1803, was marrid to Rebecca L. Mitchell of Hartford, Dec. 13, 1830, by Rev. Seth Stetson. He now resides at North Waterford. Children: David P., b. April 23, 1835, m. March 23, 1870, Martha A. Hayes; Calvin, b. Aug. 7, 1837; Zenas M., b. Feb. 17, 1839, d. July 9, 1863; Volney, b. Dec. 14, 1841, d. Jan. 31, 1863.

iii *Charles,* b. Sept. 22, 1806, m. to Mary Bancroft of Norway, Jan. 11, 1843, by Philip Bemis. Children: Oscar M., b. Nov. 3, 1843. Charles Bisbee's first wife died and he was married to Elvira B. Adley of Waterford, Aug 11, 1852, by Rev. John A. Douglass. He resides in North Waterford.

3

iv *Lewis*, born Aug. 10, 1808, resides on the old Bisbee homestead, is known as Capt. Bisbee. He was married Dec. 31, 1829, to Elizabeth Sampson of Hartford, by Bethuel Cary, Esq. Children: Amanda M., b. July 11, 1830, m. June 7, 1850, to Frederic A. Spaulding of Buckfield, by Rev. Mr. Hackett. He died June 12, 1856, and she married Rufus K. Harlow; Amarilla, b. June 13, 1832, m. Oct. 26, 1852, to William F. Bard of Hartford, d. May 29, 1853.

v *Mahala*, b. July 13, 1810, was married by Aaron Parsons, Esq., Nov. 22, 1830, to Henry E. Buck of Buckfield, and had Charles C., b. Oct. 9, 1831; Octavia, b. Jan. 9, 1834, m. Oct. 8, 1859, to Horatio A. Flagg. Henry E. Buck died Aug. 4, 1836, and Mahala, his widow, married Apr. 14, 1844, Samuel Buck, and had Cecelia, b. July 14, 1845, m. Nov. 27, 1866, Charles H. Dunham.

vi *Chloe*, b. Aug. 23, 1812, married by Charles B. Smith, Esq., July 21, 1833, to John Sampson of Middleborough, Mass., and had Adrianna, b. in Portland, Sept. 9. 1834, m. Samuel Knight; Francis M., b. Oct. 13, 1835, m. Sept. 11, 1860, Caroline Bisbee, d. May 16, 1875; Chloe, b. July 17, 1841, m. Oct. 12, 1859, to Thomas H. Sawin.

vii *Hosea B.*, b. Dec. 29, 1816, was married in 1846 to Elizabeth Clark of Woodstock, Me., and had Beulah E., b. Nov. 27, 1847. For second wife Hosea B. Bisbee married Charlotte Shaw, Sept., 1859, who had Mary, b. —— ——.

viii *Celia*, b. Feb. 19, 1823, was married Aug. 21, 1851, to Henry Snell of North Bridgewater, Mass. Left no children.

35. Rouse Bisbee married Hannah Carrell* and lived at South Paris. He subsequently lived in Belfast and Portland, but about the year 1810 he moved to Wood-

---

* Upon her headstone at North Woodstock, the name is *Cary*, inscribed on the authority of her son and only surviving child, but on the Turner, Me., records, under the head, "A list of marriages solemnized by Ichabod Bonney, Esq., from April 1, 1796, to April 1, 1797," is an entry of which the following is a *verbatim et literatim* copy: "Rouse Bisbee and Hannah Carrell, both of Butterfield, Dec. 15, 1797."

stock. He built the first mill in Woodstock, situated on the brook near Abel Bacon's house. A store and public house on a small scale were afterwards erected near, and the place was distinguished by the name of Woodstock Corner. Mr. Bisbee sold the mill to Samuel Stephens and bought John Nason's farm, where he lived a few years, keeping a small store for the accommodation of the town. He moved to North Woodstock in 1821, and was the first settler in that part of the town. Here he built a gristmill and shingle-mill, and resided here while he lived. After the incorporation of the town he was moderator of the first town meeting. He was a man of intelligence, though of marked peculiarities. He delighted in improving water-power, and every cascade which he saw suggested a dam and mill. His first wife died Feb. 28, 1850, and he married widow Mary Washburne of Paris, who survived him. He died May 3, 1852, and was buried by the side of his wife at North Woodstock. Children:

i *Sophronia*, b. Apr. 1, 1801 at South Paris, married to Joel Perham of Woodstock, and had, Sidney*, b. March 27, 1819, m. Almeda J., daughter of Lazarus and Lucy (Cole) Hathaway of Paris; Betsey G., b. March 13, 1821, m. Merrill J. Rowe of Woodstock, now of Norway; Kilbon, b. Aug. 28, 1822, m. Mary Jane Bryant of Greenwood; Joel, Jr., b. May 8, 1826, unmarried; Viania P., b. Apr. 10, 1832, m. Joseph Churchill, and resides at Norway; Cynthia A., b. June 27, 1839, m. Nov. 27, 1866, William B. Lapham of Woodstock, now of Augusta, Me. Mrs. Perham died Nov. 7, 1865, at Woodstock.

ii *Suel*, b. Aug. 13, 1802, m. Milla Whitman of Woodstock, and had, Sylvia, b. Apr. 14, 1830, m. Francis Bennett, 2d John Tibbetts; Lovina, b. Oct. 6, 1833, died unmarried; Rosilla, b. July 26,

---

* Sidney Perham was a farmer and schoolmaster in Woodstock, Me., in his early manhood. He was speaker of the Maine House of Representatives in 1855, was twice elected clerk of the Supreme Judicial Court for Oxford county, served three terms in Congress, and three years as Governor of the State.

1836. m. James F. Bird, March, 1866; Orin, b. Nov. 21, 1834, d. Jan. 25, 1874; Loanna E., b. Apr. 2, 1842, m. Dennis W. Cole of Greenwood, died 1875.   For second wife Suel Bisbee m. Sally (Curtis) Whitman, widow ot Elhanan Whitman of Waterford.

iii *Desire*, b. Jan. 31, 1805, married William Chamberlain, Jr., of Rumford, and lived and died in Woodstock.   Her children were Enos C., b. Aug. 7, 1837, m. Lizzie C. Farrar of Woodstock; Austin B., b. Jan. 16, 1842, m. Marie F. Raoiil* in Alabama, resides in Galveston, Texas.

iv *Piram*, b. Oct. 8, 1809, m. Asenath, daughter of Benjamin Swett of Bethel, and had, Hiram H. b. 1837; Benjamin S., b. Mar. 31, 1839, m. Mary F. Randall of Albany; Eliza A., b. March 30, 1844, m. Austin E. Whitman of Greenwood; Hannah C., b. Nov. 30, 1847, m. Benjamin F. Lary of Shelburne, N. H., Nov. 30, 1867; Enoch L.;† Dana B.; Catherine G.;† Sophronia P.;† Mary Francis.†

36.   Celia Bisbee, born May 7, 1764, was married to Joshua Ford of Sumner, formerly of Pembroke, Mass. Children:

i *Margaret*, b. May 28, 1786, m. Levi Cushman.

ii *Anna*, b. Nov. 9, 1787, m. Sylvanus Stevens, and had 16 children.

iii *Joshua*, Jr., b. June 27, 1789, m. Mercy Sturtevant, and had 12 children.

iv *Celia*, b. Apr. 25, 1791, m. Thaddeus Oldham; had 13 children.

v *Naoma*, b. Apr. 7, 1793, m. John Bonney, and had 13 children.

vi *Joanna*, b. Jan. 29, 1795, m. John Carpenter; 14 children.

vii *Obadiah*, b. Apr. 2, 1797, m. Hannah Sturtevant.

---

* She was drowned in the severe flood which occurred in Texas, in the spring of 1875.

†These died young.

viii *Sally*, b. July 15, 1799, m. Peter Morrill; 4 children.

ix *Angus*, b. June 20, 1801, m. Nancy Rand; 5 children.

x *Nathaniel C.*, b. Jan. 7, 1803, m. Clarissa Young; 7 children.

xi *Howland*, b. Dec. 6, 1810, m. Tamar Kidder, and had 5 children.

37. Patty Bisbee married Dr. Benjamin Bradford of Livermore, Me., in 1809. Children :

i *Flora C.*, b. Apr. 10, 1810, m. Merrit Coolidge of Portland.

ii *Osca*, b. Apr. 4, 1811, m. John W. Rigelow of Livermore, Me., Nov. 2, 1831.

iii *Celia B.*, b. Oct. 21, 1812, m. Elisha Coolidge, Oct. 17, 1843, resides in Jay, Me.

iv *Benjamin R.*, b. March 30, 1814, d. Apr. 20, 1814.

v. *Caroline S.*, b. May 4, 1815, m. Joel H. Bigelow; Nov. 2, 1835, d. Nov. 14, 1838.

vi *Benjamin R.*, b. March 26, 1817, d. June 7, 1818.

vii *Benj. F.*, b. March 8, 1819, d. June 5, 1844,

viii *Henry B.*, b. March 17, 1821, m. Nov. 3, 1847, Lydia J. Norton, lives on the Bradford homestead in Livermore.

ix *Martha B.*, b. Oct. 11, 1822, m. Joseph H. Locke, Aug. 24, 1845, reside in Fairhaven, Minn.

x *Roxanna K.*, b. Nov. 29, 1824, d. Dec. 11, 1856.

xi *Albina E.*, b. March 12, 1827, d. Nov. 30, 1845.

xii *Sarah F.*, b. July 6, 1830, d. March 9, 1847.

xiii *Algernon S.*, b. March 5, 1832, m. Ann M. Coolidge, resides in Empire, Minn.

38. Asa Bisbee in early life came from Bridgewater to North Yarmouth, Me. He was an original member of the North Yarmouth Light Infantry, which was organized in 1805. He married Oct. 8, 1815, Sarah Harvey of Pownal, who was born Aug. 20, 1793. He worked as a gunsmith and blacksmith. He served at Fort Preble in Portland harbor as Fife Major, in the war of 1812. Commenced a general trade at Yarmouth Falls in 1840, and followed this business afterwards until his decease. He was a noted mechanical genius and a natural mathematician. He died Aug. 12, 1865. Children :

   i *Susan H.*, b. May 6, 1818, m. Henry Clark Greenleaf, Jan. 20, 1848.

   ii *Ira*, b. Jan. 5, 1822, d. Aug. 9, 1826.

   iii *Francis*, b. May 8, 1824, d. May 16, 1826.

   iv *Phedyma*, b. Jan. 2, 1826, d. Aug. 29, 1826.

   v *Harriet C.*, b. Sept. 11, 1828.

   vi *Edward*, b. July 19, 1830, m. Frances E. Maxfield, d. March 20, 1871.

   vii *Sophia B.*, b. Aug. 15, 1831, d. July 4, 1857.

39.   Franklin Bisbee was said to be the best cast-steel worker in the country. At the age of 20 years, having learned his trade at Canton, Mass., he commenced work at Bridgewater for himself, manufacturing the first American cast-steel hoes and shovels. He afterwards moved to Canton, where in 1849 he commenced the manufacture of masons' trowels, having made an improvement in the ferule which he patented. He continued in this business until the time of his death, which occurred in 1868. He was married Sept. 1, 1820, to Lovina, daughter of Benjamin Bisbee of Stoughton. Children :

   i *Lovina*, b. Sept. 25, 1821, d. May 26, 1822.

---

ii *Benjamin F.*, b. March 19, 1823, m. Clara S. Kinsley of Somerville in 1853.

iii *Otis*, b. Aug. 17, 1825, m. Eliza W. Ramsdell 1844.

iv *Amanda L.*, b. May 4, 1827, m. Alanson D. Davis of Athens, Me., March 18, 1850.

v *John R.*, b. Aug. 6, 1830, d. Sept. 20, 1832.

vi *Mary E.*, b. Nov. 19, 1834.

40. Oliver Bisbee, born in Duxbury, Mass., June 10, 1762, was a ship carpenter. He married first, Huldah Simmons of Duxbury, and previous to 1790 had moved to Newmeadows, in the town of Brunswick, Me. Children :

i *Huldah*, b. Oct. 4, 1791, m. Edward McIntire. Oliver Bisbee's first wife, Huldah, died, and for second wife he married her sister, Persis Simmons, who had

ii *Rufus*,* b. Jan. 13, 1793, m. Joanna Doughty. He was living in 1875 in Brunswick.

iii *Studley*, b. July 10, 1795, m. Rachel Dickey.

iv *Hannah*, b. April 18, 1797, never married.

v *William*, b. July 4, 1799, m. Hannah Prior.

vi *Aaron*, b. Oct. 10, 1802, m. Nancy Conley.

vii *Seth*, b. Sept. 27, 1804, m. Maria Larrabee.

viii *Sarah*, b. Aug. 3, 1806, m. James Tibbetts.

* Rufus Bisbee of Brunswick, was a cooper and shoemaker. By his wife, Joanna Doughty, he had : i *William*, b. March 9, 1815; unmarried. ii *Charles W.*, b. Jan. 23, 1817; unmarried. iii *Rufus*, b. June 20, 1819; m. Maria Brown. iv *John S.*, b. July 29, 1821; m. Eliza Duston, daughter of Jesse, Jr., formerly of Rumford; he d. Aug., 1870. v. *Francis A.*, b. June 12, 1823; unmarried. vi *Edward F.*, b. March 6, 1825. vii *Elizabeth A.*, b. July 16, 1829; m. J. S. Stanwood. viii *Edward F.*, b. Apr. 3, 1832; m. Sarah Moran, 1858.

41. Benjamin Bisbee, son of Samuel of Stoughton, married Milly Vose. Children :

i *Be·jamin, Jr.*, died at Stoughton.

ii *Abner.*

iii *Lovina*, m. Franklin Bisbee (39).

iv *Otis*, m. Nancy Pope.

v. *Milly*, m. John Sulerway.

vi *Josiah B.*, never married.

vii *Hannah*, m. Jefferson Bisbee.

42. Beza Bisbee was married to Betsey Marshall by Rev. John Briggs in 1800, and died Sept. 3, 1804, aged 25 years, 5 months. His wife was the daughter of Capt. Thomas Marshall of New Bedford. Children :

i *Elijah*, b. July 4, 1804, m. Maria Soule of Plympton Jan. 2, 1825, had Susan. Elijah, Maria, Lucia S., Elizabeth and John T., and died Apr. 3, 1869.

ii *Bezai*, b. March 8, 1805, m. Catharine W. Harrub Nov. 30, 1829. March 12, 1830, he had his name changed to William Marshal Bisbee. They had Wm. Wallace, d. young; Catherine W., William Wallace. who died at sea in 1858; Elias M., Felicia H., d. young: Rachel M., Felicia M. and Eva. The father, Capt. William M. Bisbee, was lost at sea Jan. 11, 1859.

43. John Bisbee went to school in Kingston, where he was under the instruction of Rev. Martin Parris, and a classmate of Rev. W. A. Drew of Augusta. He graduated at Brown University, entering a year in advance, and always kept ahead of his class. In the language of one of his classmates, "he took to learning as naturally as a duck to the water." He graduated with the highest honors, and studied law in Taunton. He was always a serious, thoughtful man, and preferred the ministry, and having embraced Universalism he commenced to preach in Brookfield, Mass. He afterwards went to Hartford, Conn., and finally accepted a call as the successor of Rev. Russell Streeter, in Portland. He came there in July, 1827. While there he made his mark as a talented and eloquent speaker. He married Miss Ruggles of Hardwich, Mass., who subsequently married a Mr. Bugbee of Plymouth, Mass. They had two children. Rev. Mr. Bisbee died in Portland, after an illness of eight days, March 8, 1829, very much lamented. The Bisbee fraternity of Portland, perpetuates his memory. He delivered the first occasional sermon before the Maine Convention of Universalists, at its organization in 1828. Mr. Bisbee had some striking peculiarities, physically as well as mentally. His hair and beard on one side of his head and face were nearly white, on the other dark; one of his eyes was hazel, the other pale blue. When he became a man he contrived by hair dyes to color both sides of his hair alike.

Mr. Bisbee's widow is said to be now living in her second widowhood in Plymouth. Of the two children I know nothing.

NOTES.

We have stated in another place that Rouse Bisbee (35) was a person of marked peculiarities. The following little anecdote will illustrate this. While residing at North Woodstock, a dispute arose between him and a local preacher familiarly known as "the elder," who worked at blacksmithing, about the ownership of an anvil. The anvil had changed hands several times, each party taking it whenever he had an opportunity. Mr. Bisbee grew weary of this by-play, and one day when "the elder" had carried off the anvil, he walked into the shop of the latter and without commencing a war of words, he simply placed a stick which he carried in his hand against the forge, and walked out without saying a word. The stick was an elder sprout, not of the sweet variety, but of the other kind, and this was Mr. Bisbee's method of showing the minister the kind of "elder" he considered him.

John Bisbee (32) was not over-scrupulous respecting his dress or personal appearance, though he was in comfortable circumstances. The following story related of him may or may not be true. It is said that on one occasion, clad in home-spun, he went to Portland with a load of furs which he found it difficult to dispose of without taking his pay in goods. He urged that he must have some money to pay his taxes, and finally the dealer closed the bargain by promising to pay him money enough for that purpose. Mr. Bisbee then stepped out and called in the collector of Sumner, who happened to be in the city, when it was found that the entire amount he was to receive for his furs was insufficient to cancel his taxes. The dealer acknowledged the corn and paid over the money.

Hopestill Bisbee son of Hopestill (21) settled in Middleboro', Mass., where he married widow Betsey Purrington, whose maiden name was Clark. He had two sons viz: Hopestill and Alden; their posterity is in Middieboro' and vicinity.

As a race the Bisbee's are distinguished for their mechanical ingenuity, and especially for their skill in working iron and steel. A larger per cent. of them are blacksmiths than of any other family I know, except perhaps the family of Leonard.

Elisha Bisbee, probably (12), was one of the petitioners to the General Court in 1735, for a grant of land in the District of Maine, afterwards incorporated as Gray.

In the Genealogy of the Lewis Family it is stated that Daniel, only son of Rev. Daniel Lewis, married Sarah, daughter of Elisha Bisbee (5) of Hingham.

Rev. J. H. Bisbee wrote the Ecclesiastical History of Worthington, Mass.

In his will Thomas Bisbee, (1) the emigrant, directed that his body should be buried at the East end of the church in Sudbury.

APPENDIX.

ELISHA BISBEE, ESQ.

The following communication from Ellis Ames, Esq., of Canton, Mass., to the Old Colony Memorial, contains some facts respecting Elisha Bisbee, Esq., (12) and his descendents, which are worth preserving here. We believe that Mr. Ames claims to be a descendent. We omit the first part of the communication, which relates principally to other matters.

In the fall of 1848, the writer fell in with Mr. Benjamin Bisbee of Stoughton, then 89 years of age, and inquired of him from whom he was named; to which he replied, from his uncle Benjamin Bisbee, who was killed at the battle of Lake George in 1755; that his uncle Benjamin and Samuel Bisbee, his father, were sons of Elisha Bisbee, Esq., of Pembroke, who died in 1737; that his uncle on departing for the army after his enlistment, went up to the window of his brother Samuel's house and requested that if he (his brother) should have a son born, to name him Benjamin, and that he was named accordingly at his birth; that by one Packard of North Bridgewater, who was in the same company with his uncle Benjamin, he was told that his uncle Benjamin Bisbee was slightly wounded in the leg, and was thereby thrown into convulsions and died about sunset of the day of the battle, of the lock-jaw; and that he, Packard, buried him near a tree, which he marked with the initials of his name. On the decease of Mr. Benjamin Bisbee, in October, 1849, a biographical sketch of him was prepared, which was published in the January number, 1850, of the *New England Genealogical Register*, on pages 99 and 100, in which the account of his uncle Benjamin Bisbee having been killed at the battle of Lake George, and his being named after him, is narrated. His fellow-soldier and his brother and his connections thought that he died of lock-jaw, induced by the slight wound he received, and do not seem to have been aware that his death was caused by a poisoned bullet.

On looking into the account of the administrator, (his brother, Samuel Bisbee,) in the well-known handwriting of Shepard Fiske,

Esq., of Bridgewater, allowed in the Plymouth County Probate Court, January 2, 1758, we find this item, viz:

"To a journey to Boston (and time in waiting on the Province treasurer) to receive the wages due the estate," being the item for services in collecting the back pay of the government. This account was allowed by John Cushing, Esq., Judge of Probate for Plymouth County, who was also at the same time a Judge of the Supreme Court of Massachusetts, and who was the father of Hon. William Cushing, afterwards Chief Justice of Massachusetts, and subsequently for twenty-one years one of the Judges of the Supreme Court of the United States, and who was commissioned Chief Justice of the United States.

Let us see more fully who was this Benjamin Bisbee, who was killed at the battle of Lake George, Sept. 8, 1755.

Elisha Bisbee, Esq., of Pembroke, was a lawyer, who was born in Hingham and moved to Pembroke, and represented that town in the General Court about ten years, the last year being the political year 1736—1737.

Upon examining the grave-stones in the old burying-ground in Pembroke, we find one with the following inscription, to wit:

> "HERE LIES YE BODY OF
> ELISHA BISBEE, ESQ.,
> AGED 49 YEARS & 12 DAYS.
> DIED MARCH YE 13TH, 1737."

He was buried beside the grave of his son, named after him or for him, as appears by a small grave-stone, with this inscription, viz:

> "ELISHA, SON TO ELISHA & SARAH BISBEE,
> AGED 5 YEARS & 2 MONTHS.
> DIED AUGUST 20, 1723."

Beside him also was buried his own mother, as appears by a gravestone larger than that over his own grave, with this inscription, viz:

> "HERE LIES THE BODY OF
> MRS. MARY BISBEE,
> WIFE TO ELISHA BISDEE,
> OF HINGHAM, GENTL.
> DIED APRIL 16, 1737,
> IN THE 82D YEAR OF
> HER AGE.

Sarah, the widow of Elisha Bisbee, Esq., subsequently married Mr. Josiah Williams, of West Bridgewater, the great-grandfather of the late Hon. Reuel Williams of Maine. Josiah Williams died in 1770, his dwelling-house still standing in a good state of preservation. Upon her second marriage to Mr. Williams. as his second wife, her sons, Benjamin and Samuel, moved with her to West Bridgewater, and from that place her son, Benjamin Bisbee, enlisted into the Provincial army in the spring of 1755. Samuel, the brother of Benjamin, moved from West Bridgewater to Stoughton in 1764, and there lived and died in the year 1800.

Elisha Bisbee, Esq., practiced law and attended Court in several counties, his name appearing as counsel on the record. He was the identical person appearing at the bar in Worcester in 1732, of whom the late learned Joseph Willard, Esq., in his history of the bar of Worcester County, seems to have known only enough to head the list of the ancient lawyers at that bar with the name of

"ELISHA BISBEE, 1732."

Elisha Bisbee was a member of the General Court of so much consequence as to have been, at one time chairman of the Committee of the House of representatives on the important subject of the Governor's salary, when, on account of the interference of the King and his ministers on that subject, the Province was much agitated. That Elisha Bisbee had business in Worcester County appears by the fact that, at the time of his decease, he owned lands in the town of Hardwicke, in that county as seen by his inventory, wherein is this item:

"LAND IN LAMBSTOWN, £25;"

for we familiarly know that the territory of Hardwicke went under the name of *Lambstown* until it was incorporated by the name of Hardwicke on January 10, 1739.

Elisha Bisbee was last elected the representative to the General Court from Pembroke, at the spring election of 1736. He took his seat as such at Boston at the opening of the first session on the last Wednesday of May, 1736. The first session adjourned on July 6, 1736, to Sept. 8, 1736, and was further adjourned by the Proclamation of the Governor to Nov. 25, 1736, when the Legislature assembled and continued in session until on February 4, 1737, when it adjourned to the 13th April, 1737, before which time, by Proclamation from the Governor, the General Court was dissolved and the members discharged from any further attendance.

That Mr. Bisbee was active, the first session, notwithstanding he was sick of a settled consumption, is evident, inasmuch as, on the 4th day of June, 1736, he got through the House a grant to the town of Pembroke of one thousand acres of unappropriated lands of the Province for the use of that town, *"the better to enable them to keep a grammar school therein."*

We would like to see a full biographical sketch of Elisha Bisbee, Esq., and some account of his genius and talents; but, doubtless, it is too late to attempt it. Numerous legal documents have we seen in his hand-writing proving his skill as a draftsman, and the records of the Courts in Plymouth, and other counties, show that he often tried causes at the bar, from which it is necessarily inferred that he had forensic skill, and was of the first class of the lawyers of the day.

We copy from the original in our possession, a letter written by him to his wife, while attending, as the representative of Pembroke, the June session, 1736, of the General Court at Boston, which shows the nature of the sickness with which he was then afflicted, and of which doubtless he died the March following:

"MY DEAR:

These with my love come to let you know that I hope in about ten days to see you; God willing. As to my health I can say but little about it; but am much as I was. When the weather is very hot I lie by, and when the air is thick I dare not go out, but am as careful as I can. I have got on a stomach plaster again; I hope it is of some service. I shall, I think, bring you some flax and cotton wool; but they are very dear. Flax I cannot have under two shillings and five pence and take a good quantity. As to sheep's wool, don't neglect to go to John Little, Esq., claim his promise, and tell him you must have what you have occasion for, &c. Give my duty to my mother, my love to my children, sister and all friends, which, in haste, is all at present.

From your loving husband, ELISHA BISBEE.

. Boston, June ye 4th, 1736.   To Sarah Bisbee."

The grave-stones show that his aged mother survived Mr. Bisbee but thirty-four days. Probably her death was hastened by grief for the death of her son, in whose family she, a widow, was then living. With what affection he regarded her the letter above bears witness.

The month of August and the first week in Sept. 1755, were a sad time in Massachusetts and throughout the English Provinces in North America. Braddock's army had been utterly defeated on the 9th of July previous, and our frontier settlements for hundreds of miles were by reason of that defeat abandoned, and the inhabitants had fled eastward, losing their property; in dread of the tomahawk and scalping-knife. Indeed at that time it was seriously apprehended by some of our ablest men that the entire English settlements in North America might be subverted and extinguished by the combined efforts of the French and Indians. The victory at Lake George was hailed with great joy as a set-off to Braddock's defeat, and revived the drooping spirits of the people.

This article cannot be devoid of interest in that we thereby learn the pedigree and the home and connections of a brave soldier from Plymouth County, who fell in battle, "at the crisis of a nation's peril," and who is worthy of grateful remembrance; and we are glad that the author has mentioned his name, (although misspelled in the printing*) and so given occasion for bringing his name out from obscurity to the notice of succeeding generations dwelling in the vicinity of his birth and residence.

---

* Mr. Ames here refers to a published account of the battle, which speaks of the wounding of one *Brisbee*, which should have read *Bisbee*.

RECORD MADE BY HOPESTILL BISBEE, Jr.

The following brief record was made by Hopestill Bisbee, Jr.(21) of Rochester, Mass., and is still preserved in the family. It will be noticed that he is not correct in all points :

"I moved from Plympton to Rochester, Mass., in 1771. My father's grandfather came from the North of England, he. and his wife in their younger years, and settled in Marshfield or Scituate. They had two sons, John and Hopestill.* John had six sons and two daughters. His sons' names were John, Elijah, Aaron, Elisha, Moses and Hopestill; the names of his daughters, Martha and Mary. Hopestill was a lawyer, and called the honest lawyer. I do not know whether he had any children. My father Hopestill was born April 16th, 1702 old style, and died March 17th, 1784; Hannah his wife, daughter of Wm. Churchill of Plympton, born Oct., 23, 1707, died Oct. 26, 1797. I was born May 20, 1741."

BISBEES IN THE WAR FOR INDEPENDENCE.

I find the following names of Bisbees on the original muster rolls which are preserved in the archives of Massachusetts. Perhaps this list does not include all who were in the service. Some of the names given here are not found in the preceding Family Records :

Aaron,	Elijah,	John,	Reuben,
Abner,	Elisha,	Jonah,	Samuel,
Asaph,	Ezra,	Joshua,	Stephen,
Charles,	Gamaliel,†	Jotham,	Zebulon.
Ebenezer,	George,	Luther,—	
Edward,	Hopestill,	Noah,	
Eleazer,	Isaac,‡	Oliver,	

* It will be noticed here that the writer refers to Elisha Bisbee (2) as his emigrant ancestor, and in fact he was, though he came over from England with his father Thomas. I have come across similar traditions in other branches of the family.

† Gamaliel Bisbee was of Pembroke, Mass., where by wife Ruth ———, he had : i *Severus*, b. Nov. 19, 1781; ii *Aretas*, b. June 19, 1790; iii *Orpha*, b. Apr. 3, 1793; iv *Stetson*, b. Jan. 20, 1797.

‡ Isaac Bisbee was the son of Jarius Bisbee and of Susannah, his wife, and was born in Pembroke Feb. 23, 1753. His brother, Wadsworth Bisbee, was born July 4, 1754. I know nothing more of these families.

BISBEES IN THE WAR OF THE REBELLION.

The following persons bearing the name of Bisbee, are found in the Reports of the Adjutant General of Maine, as having served in the late war. These are probably all descendents of Charles Bisbee (15). Some of this descent served in regiments outside of the State, with whose names I have not been furnished:

Name.	Residence.	Regiment.
Charles M.,		Coast Guards.
Dennis, Jr.,		"
Elisha S.,		4th Maine,
Elisha T.,	Portland,	29th "
Forest E.,	Auburn,	32d "
Jesse D.,	Brunswick,	7th Maine Battery.
Leander D.,		6th " "
Robert,	Calais,	16th Maine.
Levi B.,	Belfast;	4th "
Horatio, Jr.,	Peru,	9th "
Elisha S.,	"	9th "
Lewis C.,	Canton,	16th "
Eliab G.,	Sumner,	1st "
Hannibal, Jr.,	Peru,	1st Maine Cavalry.
Walter C.,	Albany,	23d Maine.
Volney, 2d,	Waterford,	23d "
David P.,	"	23d "
Albert P.,	"	23d "
Joseph B.,	Warren,	24th "
John A.,	"	24th "
George D.,	Peru,	16th "
Orrin S.,	Greenwood,	27th "
Charles D.,	Biddeford,	27th "
Andrew B.,	Norridgewock,	7th "
Hiram B.,	Peru,	9th "
Ira W.,	Paris,	9th "
Elisha F.,	Canton,	9th "
Elisha T.,	Sumner,	10th "

www.ingramcontent.com/pod-product-compliance
Lightning Source LLC
Chambersburg PA
CBHW021554270326
41931CB00009B/1203